Toilet Trivia

More Mountainous Doo for You

250 Amazing Fun Facts, Shorts Reads, Geographical Oddities, and Amusing Anecdotes

Adicus Abbott

Toilet Trivia

Summary: Collection of sports, history, geography and human interest trivia. Keywords: (1) trivia, (2) trivia books, (3) sports trivia, (4) bathroom humor, (5) fun facts (6) anecdotes, (7) short reads

Published in the United States

ISBN-13: 978-1981617173

ISBN-10: 1981617175

"Well ain't this place a geographical oddity!
Two weeks from everywhere!"

George Clooney

O Brother, Where Art Thou?

Table of Contents

Bathroom Facts, Figures, and Humor

Bathrooms are like geographical oddities. When you need one bad, they're all two weeks from everywhere.

Even at home, bathrooms are often tucked "down the hall and around the corner," or hidden in the back recesses of a master bedroom. And as for size, have you ever wondered why the most important room in your entire house is also the smallest?

Think about that the next time you find yourself tap dancing at the front door as you fumble with your keys and struggle to think of geographical oddities, the gross domestic product of China, the population of Upper Mongolia, and a hundred other non-bathroom related thoughts.

*****

In 1949, an Air Force engineer named Edward Murphy encountered a problem with a deceleration project he was working on. He noticed one of the other engineers had made a mistake, and claimed, "If there's anything that can be done wrong, trust him to do it."

Over time, this phrase morphed into what we now recognize as Murphy's Law: "If anything can go wrong, it will."

So, how does Murphy's Law pertain to uncontrollable urges and mad dashes to the most sanctified of sanctuaries?

Easy. I call it Abbott's Law:

"Invariably, the stronger the urge, the more likely you will discover the bathroom is in use."

*****

According to research conducted in Britain, a survey of 2,500 adults found that men spend on average, one hour and 45 minutes per week on the toilet. Excluding the obligatory wait times in long stadium and concert hall public facilities, women spend less time on the toilet than men, at a mere 85 minutes per week.

With a little extrapolation, you'll see a man spends about 91 hours per year on the toilet. That is enough time to complete at least 2 college courses in a residential college program, and as many as 11 courses in an online program.

Like most of the statistics used in this book, *averages* neglect to reveal the true picture, and often hide the extreme outliers in any given set of data. For example, I know for a fact that as a shift worker, I often spent at least one and half hours per 8 hours shift on the toilet. Anything less and you would have the Shop Steward on your butt for making the other guys in the shop look bad. I also know that my son, who prides himself in doing everything fast, spends less than three minutes on the toilet per day.

*****

The MacAdoos — my next-door neighbors in Guthrie, Oklahoma — were another extreme example of odd behavior. I can remember the sound of a sledge hammer smashing a hole in the MacAdoos' kitchen wall to make way for a bathroom and their first indoor toilet like it was yesterday. I was mad because Neil Armstrong was flying to the Moon and their pounding and sawing was interrupting transmissions from Mission Control.

In contrast, around 800 years before the birth of Christ, King Minos of Crete installed what may be the first indoor flushing toilet in his palace. Little is known about the inventor of this toilet, nor whether or not the toilet met environmental standards for gallons of water used per flush, or who may have been invited and who may have been expressly prohibited from using the wooden contraption. Either way, the concept did not catch on, as it was not until 1594 that Sir John Harrington developed a flushing toilet for Queen Elizabeth.

While absent from the historical record, current toilet usage, personal experience, and the enviable wealth of plumbers worldwide, suggests the first plumber in the history of forever first forced his hand into a clogged toilet within approximately 30 minutes after the installation of the queen's indoor commode.

*****

Humans are by nature, creatures of habit. And the one habit we did not relinquish lightly was how and where we toileted. In fact, as recently as the 1960s, many homes in rural America lacked indoor plumbing. Sure, most housewives had access to a water pump or city provided tap water in their kitchens by 1960. However, the idea of toileting in the house was still seen as less than sanitary.

Fortunately, the creation of vented pipes, bathroom fans, air fresheners, and a widely accepted practice known today as a "courtesy flush," won the day.

*****

As of the 2010 Census, the U.S. Census Bureau reported 99.36 percent of the nations' population had indoor plumbing, leaving well over 1 million people without access to a flushing indoor toilet.

Shocking as that may seem, the outbreak of hepatitis A in many major west coast cities in 2017 has been attributed to the homeless community's lack of access to basic sanitation. Homeless people, who by definition do not have a toilet in their home, live, eat, sleep, and yes, toilet, in less than ideal places. According to the National Alliance to End Homelessness, approximately 564,000 people are homeless in America at any given time,

That accounts for a lot of human waste, and a lot of missed opportunities to prevent the spread of communicable diseases. To put it mildly, on the streets of San Francisco, a city well accustomed to throngs of homeless street walkers soiling the doorways of homes and businesses, we are one zombie virus short of a global pandemic.

*****

According to the Bureau of Labor Statistics, the median income for plumbers is $49,000 annually, or about 14 grand more than the median income for all occupations nationally. Again, outliers skew the data, but many licensed plumbers earn between $70,000 and $90,000 per year. In fact, my neighbor drives a pick-up with his plumber info on the door during the day. In the evening, he takes his wife to dinner in a Maserati, and often spends the weekends cruising the mountain highways of California on his Harley-Davidson. He does not have a high school diploma or college degree. But he does have a year of vocational school under his belt, and proudly displays his plumber's license in his garage man cave.

*****

We've all heard of plumber's butt, right? But have you actually ever seen it?

Personally, I thought it was a myth. One of those old wives' tales perpetuated by a little old lady from Peoria who hired a homeless guy with no belt and sagging britches to unclog her kitchen sink in exchange for a cup of hot tea and slice of yellow pound cake.

And then I had a problem and needed a plumber.

The man walked into my house, assessed the problem, and hunched down to reset my garbage disposal. And there it was. Plumber's butt. It wasn't a myth.

Upon further inquiry, I discovered plumber's butt is so common, scientists have actually given it a scientific name. It's called, *intergluteal cleft*.

Knowing the scientific name of things helps when you're in therapy.

*****

On the messier side of things, you may be interested to learn the use of paper products in the toilet is not universal. Around 75 percent of the world's population—over 4 billion—do not use toilet paper. Some of these people prefer to use water to clean their backsides, while many others simply *let it ride.*

*****

So, just how much paper does it take to get the job done? On average, Americans use 57 sheets of toilet paper per day, which includes using toilet paper for a variety of chores beyond mere backside cleaning. Nationally, that adds up to over 400 million miles of rolled paper every year. To offset the costs of keeping our prized water closets stocked, 7 percent of Americans admit to stealing paper products from public restrooms. On a side note, during World War II, rationing of toilet paper in Great Britain limited toilet paper usage to one sheet per day.

*****

When it comes to toilets and toileting, there is no end to human curiosity. Recently, a research group spent over $100,00 to find the answer to the life changing question: Do people put their toilet paper on the spindle with the flap in front or behind? As it turns out, 75 percent of people prefer to hang their toilet paper with the flap hanging out.

There was no evidence the researchers asked how many people didn't even bother to put their toilet paper on the spindle. In my household, the paper is consumed so quickly, I've long since resigned myself to the *why even bother* crowd.

*****

So, do you flush the toilet while still sitting on it? Or do you prefer to stand up and flush?

Your toilet may be different than mine, but in my experience, if you flush the toilet while you're still implanted on the seat, prepare for a cold, sewage enriched, shower. Two thirds of the world agrees with me, leaving over 33 percent of toilet flushers in the *flush while seated* category.

*****

There was a time, not too long ago, when reading was the most popular form of passing the time on the john. This has been replaced with talking and texting on one's cell phone, with up to 75 percent of people claiming to routinely using their phones on the john. As you might expect, this has also led to disaster, as over 7 million phones per year fall into the toilet.

This statistic hits rather close to home, as I recently lost my prized flip phone to the toilet after placing it in my shirt pocket. After flushing the toilet, I leaned over to drop the seat in a gentleman's gesture towards the ladies in my home. As I leaned forward to set the seat down, my phone plopped into the toilet. Knowing plumbers cash in on the propensity towards flushing our troubles down the drain, I fished the phone out with the toilet brush and a hunk of toilet paper. Later that day I discovered flip phones are no longer cool, and graduated to a Smart Phone that is currently doing its best to make me feel stupid.

*****

Because you asked, I'm here to tell you…some of us are crumple bots, and some of us are folders.

A crumple bot wads his or her paper in a baseball shaped mass before use. A folder neatly doubles and triples his or her paper into a neat stack. According to secret NSA cameras (how else do they get this info?), 40 percent of people fold their paper, and 60 percent of us crumple. Both methods seem to work, but in my opinion, the crumpled technique is more effective due to the random debris gathering features of crumpled paper, versus the smooth, folded approach.

*****

I mentioned the loss of my prized flip phone while dropping the toilet seat in a gentlemanly gesture to the ladies of my household. Guess what? Putting the toilet seat down is not just a kind gesture…it will also keep you out of the emergency room. As it turns out, *South Park* was right. People (mostly women) get hurt falling into toilets that do not have the seat down. In fact, up to 85 percent of all bathroom injuries are toilet related falls due to inconsiderate men leaving the seat in the full and upright position, and over 40,000 people per year claim injuries sustained from falling off the toilet.

And don't think toilet accidents only happen in trailer parks and prisons. In 1760, King George II of England reportedly died as a result of a fall from his toilet.

*****

Most toilet paper is white. But don't be surprised to find pink toilet paper in your hotel bathroom in Paris. The French prefer pink over white colored toilet paper.

*****

And just when you thought your bathroom was the last bastion of privacy…think again. When you invite guests into your home, know this: 70 percent of them — that's 7 out of 10 for those of you who learned math under the new common core system — are going to snoop. They're going to poke their noses into your medicine cabinet, check out Aunt Flo's essentials, and discover your inner most digestive secrets, as well as your preferred brand of hemorrhoid cream.

Is there nothing sacred in this world? Better yet, can you think of any interesting and clever ways to have fun with this human propensity to snoop? Personally, I like the idea of storing a half empty box of novelty, super-sized condoms in the medicine cabinet. But, alas, my wife objects to this flagrant exhibition of over compensation.

Earth, Wind, and Fire

Once the paperwork is finished and you venture beyond the claustrophobic confines of your bathroom, a world of over 7.5 billion people, divided among 195 nations and averaging 129 people per square mile, awaits you.

*****

But don't wait too long. By 2050, the United Nations predicts the world population will rise to 9.5 billion.

Personally, based on the increased traffic in front of my house over the past 10 years, and my daughter's inclination to single-handedly fill every vacant slot of the family Bible's birth recordings page, I suspect that growth forecast is low.

*****

Either way, the study of population statistics is known as demographics, and can be quite revealing about who we are. Did you know:

- China and India combined have over 2.5 billion people.
- The largest ethnic group in the world is Han Chinese.
- More people speak Mandarin than any other language.
- 17 percent of the world's adult population cannot read.
- We tend to cluster in urban areas. By 2007, over 50 percent of the world's population had migrated off the farm and into the city.
- Populations remain stable at a birthrate of 2.1 children per woman. Worldwide, the current birthrate stands at 2.5.
- Gender wise, and excluding any tendencies towards transgender identifications, the world's population is almost exactly divided between male and female—unless you are attending an all-boys or all-girls school—which may tend to skew your perception of the world.
- Over 25 percent of the world's population are children, with people over the age of 65 accounting for less than 8 percent. Again, your perception of this number may vary, depending upon whether you hang out around day care centers or all-you-can-eat buffets.
- Despite wars and flu epidemics, the world's population tripled in the 20th century, from 1.65 billion in 1900, to just under 6 billion by 1999.

*****

In America, the Census Bureau reports a population of 323,127,513, as of July, 2016.

- 76.9% White
- 13.3% Black or African American
- 17.8% Hispanic
- 5.7% Asian
- 1.3% American Indian

*****

How far do you drive to get to work? In Southern California, a commute from affordable housing areas outside Los Angeles can entail a 2 hour drive — one way — depending upon traffic conditions on the 405 and whether or not Kim Kardashian is in town.

On average, Americans drive 25 minutes to get to work.

*****

While functional illiteracy rates may detract from these numbers, the Census Bureau reports 86 percent of adults in America are literate. Which implies they can read well enough to find their name in the phone book, or download a free cell phone app in two out of three attempts.

Interestingly, the Census Bureau also reports that 86 percent of adults in America have a high school diploma, which suggests if you can read, you can graduate. 30 percent of all adults in America have a four year, or higher, college degree, and 8 percent of U.S. adults holds a graduate degree. 39 percent of these degrees are conferred in business, health, and social science fields, and 5 percent are in engineering fields.

Worldwide, 7 percent of all people have a college degree.

*****

The circumference of the Earth is 24,901 miles at the Equator. This may sound big, but keep in mind, the planet is 70 percent ocean. By the time you also subtract the uninhabitable polar regions, everything we know and recognize as home is confined to a rather small junk of dirt in the incomprehensible vastness of a lonely universe.

There are 57,308,738 square miles of land surface on Earth. Sadly, 33 percent of this area is desert, and 24 percent is mountainous, leaving 24,642,757 square miles, or 15.7 billion acres, of habitable land.

*****

While browsing vacant lots in my community, I noticed the real estate sales people had begun to market their lots by the square foot, and not by the acre, half acre, or quarter acre.

Admittedly, the price of $22 per square foot sounded like a good deal. But then I did the math. An acre contains 43,560 square feet. Which means the price per acre of the vacant lot in front of me was $958,320. Sure, the lot included a curb, paved road access, and buried utilities. But from the property's humble origins as a carrot farm, the leap to nearly $1 million per acre seemed steep.

By the way, the land did not include water or mineral rights. Just a patch of dirt. Within a year the carrot farm within one mile of my home had been transformed into a housing development, and despite my misgivings, the new grocery store built on the corner of the development has become my go to spot for toilet paper supplies.

*****

The Equator divides the planet in half, into equally sized northern and southern hemispheres. The Equator and the Tropic of Cancer and the Tropic of Capricorn are imaginary lines drawn on the globe to mark the tilt of the Earth.

- The Tropic of Cancer lies 23.5 degrees north of the Equator.
- The Tropic of Capricorn lies 23.5 degrees south of the Equator.

The tropics mark the latitude on Earth where the sun is directly overhead at noon on the two solstices. The northern tropic (Cancer) has the sun directly overhead at noon on June 21. The southern tropic (Capricorn) has the sun directly overhead at noon on December 21.

These dates mark the beginning of winter on December 21, and the beginning of summer on June 21 in the northern hemisphere. Down under, the seasons are reversed, with summer starting December 21, and winter beginning on June 21.

*****

Brazil is the only country in the world that has both the Equator and a tropic cross through its territory.

*****

The Amazon River is the largest river in the world, in terms of volume, with 209,000 cubic meters of water per second. This incredible water flow is greater than the combined total of the next 7 largest rivers on the planet. Its headwaters are located in Peru. The Amazon Estuary, where it flows into the Atlantic Ocean, is 202 miles wide.

Reportedly, no bridges cross the Amazon.

*****

In terms of discharge volume, the top ten rivers on the planet are:

- Amazon
- Congo
- Orinoco
- Ganges
- Madeira
- Yangtze
- Negro
- Rio de la Plata
- Yenisei
- Brahmaputra

In terms of length, the top ten longest rivers on the planet are:

- Amazon
- Nile
- Yangtze
- Mississippi
- Yenisei
- Yellow
- Ob-Irtysh
- Parana-Rio de la Plata
- Congo
- Amur

*****

John Wesley Powell led a team of explorers down the Colorado River and through the Grand Canyon in 1869. At the time, it was believed massive vortices sucked the Colorado River into the Earth somewhere within the Grand Canyon.

Prior to Powell's transit of the Grand Canyon, riding the rapids into the canyon was considered suicide. At the height of the water's rage, two members of his team decided to abandon the suicidal run and attempted to "climb" out of the canyon.

They were never heard from again.

*****

When not rafting the great rivers of the world, outdoor enthusiasts devote their time and energy to planting flags on the summits of the planet's tallest mountains.

When asked why he chose to climb Mount Everest, Sir Edmund Hillary reportedly said, "Because it is there."

By the way…Hillary was the first man to ever reach the Everest summit on May 29, 1953. The cigarette smoking Sherpa guide, Tenzing Norgay, who carried Hillary's gear to the summit, received little recognition for his amazing feat.

*****

The ten highest mountains on Earth include:

- Everest, 29,029 feet
- K2, 28,251 feet
- Kangchenjunga, 28,169 feet
- Lhoste, 27,940 feet
- Makalu, 27,838 feet
- Cho Oyu, 26,864 feet
- Dhaulagiri 26,795 feet
- Manaslu, 26,781 feet
- Nanga Parbat, 26,660 feet
- Annapurna, 26,545 feet

All of these mountain peaks are part of the Himalayas, lending credence to their designation as the "Top of the Earth."

*****

Mountain climbers are proud, ego driven people, and tabulate their conquests like Billy the Kid notched his pistol.

But in the mountain climbing community, no climber is worth his or her salt until he or she has conquered the seven highest summits of the seven continents. The prized *Seven Summits* actually includes nine summits:

- Denali, North America
- Aconcagua, South America
- Vinson, Antarctica
- Mount Blanc, Europe
- Kilimanjaro, Africa
- Elbrus, Eurasia
- Everest, Asia
- Puncak, Indonesia
- Kosciuszko, Australia

The first person to complete the challenge was Richard Bass in 1985. Reportedly, a man with time on his hands named Bill Allen has done it twice.

*****

A thick climbing rope dangles from a precipice just short of the Matterhorn summit. To this day, climbers rely upon the rope to help them reach the top. My hat is off to the climber who first installed the rope. He either had wings, or massive dangling man parts.

You Are What You Eat

Some of us eat to live…and some of us live to eat. Either way, humans, like all animals, are programmed to eat. We can't help it. Hunger pangs and the irresistible urge to consume food is in our genetic coding.

As the wide variety of ethnic and culturally based food choices available in any town or city with more than one horse corral indicates, there is an endless list of food options available to suit any taste or personal preference.

This section explores that variety — in graphic detail.

*****

In America, the hamburger evolved from a slab of ground beef slapped between two slices of white bread, to a gourmet meal of beef, lettuce, tomato, onions, pickles, and cheese on a grilled artisan bun. The addition of secret sauces—primarily made from mayonnaise and ketchup combinations—adds to the allure.

*****

A man named Fletcher Davis from Athens, Texas, claims to have created the first hamburger in the 1880s. According to Fletcher, his sandwich featured fried ground beef served on bread with a swab of mustard.

*****

During the late 1700s an English Lord known as the Earl of Sandwich was famous for his long bouts of gambling. According to legend, the Earl of Sandwich would not break off his gambling to eat, and requested his servants bring him a simple meal of a slab of meat nestled between two slices of bread.

His gambling partners caught on to the idea, and asked their servants to, "give me a Sandwich."

An alternative version of this story holds that the Earl of Sandwich was so dedicated to his work in the Admiralty, he would not break off for meals, and requested the meat and bread concoction brought to his desk where he could eat with one hand while writing letters with the other.

*****

Two hundred and fifty years later I was able to personally witness this one-handed deftness when my truck driving partner managed to routinely eat a foot-long *Subway* sandwich while driving a Peterbilt tractor pulling a 53-foot trailer through town, negotiating turns, stops, and ten gears while happily munching on his loaded cold cut trio on Italian bread with roasted garlic. To his credit, I never saw an olive or chunk of onion hit the floor of the truck cab.

*****

Incidentally, the Hawaii Islands were originally known as the Sandwich Islands, named by Captain Cook in honor of the Earl when the Earl served as the First Lord of the Admiralty...a position later held by a controversial, and in some eyes grossly incompetent, Winston Churchill, during World War I.

*****

In the world of sandwiches and hamburgers, the *Big Mac* is perhaps the most widely known. A McDonald's franchise owner named Jim Delligatti from Uniontown, Pennsylvania, created the first *Big Mac* in 1967.

Three days later the recipe for his special sauce found its way to a deep state online DARPA bulletin board, and into my secret file of all things edible.

Adicus Abbott's

<u>Special Sauce Recipe</u>

1/2 cup mayonnaise

4 teaspoons sweet pickle relish

1 teaspoon white vinegar

1/8 teaspoon salt

2 tablespoons French dressing

1 tablespoon finely minced white onion

1 teaspoon sugar

*****

If you grew up in the 1970s, you may have had the *Big Mac* advertising jingle permanently implanted in your brain. In case you've forgotten, it went like this: "Two all beef patties, special sauce, lettuce, cheese, pickles, onions on a sesame seed bun."

And just in case eating a *Big Mac* does not satisfy your *Big Mac Attack*, you can fully immerse yourself in *Big Mac* trivia by visiting the *Big Mac Museum* in North Huntington, Pennsylvania.

*****

Admittedly, there are better hamburgers to be had than a *Big Mac*. But even if you dislike McDonald's food, you may find it utterly delectable compared to what some people choose to eat for lunch.

I was born and raised in the Mojave Desert, so you may not find it surprising when I say, I fear, loathe, and despise scorpions. And just so you know, the scorpions who found their way into our shoes, beneath our beds, and under the bales of hay in my dad's hay barn, were bark scorpions — the worst kind of scorpion in America.

Anyway, this is not about scorpion stings, but the eating of scorpions. Imagine my revulsion when a tour guide pointed to a stall in a Beijing market and said, "Fried scorpion, anyone?"

No thanks.

The Chinese believe scorpion is a delicacy and display them in the marketplace skewered on sticks like beef on a shish kabob.

I love Chinese food, but I think I'll stick with orange chicken, vegetable egg rolls, and mountains of chow mein.

*****

Chow mein is a well-known noodle and vegetable dish served in virtually every Chinese restaurant in the world. But are you sure you are not eating lo mein?

Both chow mein and lo mein are made from egg noodles with a bit of wheat flour. Traditionally, chow mein noodles are fried and tend to be drier and crispier than lo mein noodles. Lo mein noodles are tossed, as the word "lo" suggests in Mandarin.

As it turns out, I prefer my egg noodles fried and slightly crisp, as opposed to soft, boiled, and tossed. Several years ago I stopped going to my favorite Chinese buffet restaurant because the noodles changed from *chow* to *lo*. I didn't realize at the time that a new cook in the restaurant was making lo mein, in place of the old cook's preference for chow mein.

The fried version of chow mein is popular in Chinese take-out, but traditional Chinese food favors the lo mein, soft noodle style.

*****

Chinese food first became popular in America during the 1849 California Gold Rush. During that time, thousands of men struggled to find an inexpensive alternative to their boring and nutritionally inadequate diet of hard tack crackers and beef jerky.

In the 1800s men were unaccustomed to cooking for themselves, and traditionally relied upon the women around them to deal with such matters. But in the Gold Fields of California, women were scarce. In fact, there were close to 100 men for every 8 women in California at the time. And this number dropped to a fraction of 1 percent in the mining camps scattered throughout the High Sierras.

Entrepreneurial Chinese cooks saw an opportunity before them and set up shops to feed the miners for a fraction of the cost the miners paid for basic food items like flour and eggs.

Using a huge variety of vegetables and some chicken, creative Chinese cooks developed the first truly American fast food. They called it chop suey.

Years later, chop suey lost its appeal as diners demanded more authentic Chinese cuisine, and not the creation of an Americanized Chinese cook in a California gold mining camp.

*****

On a side note, fancy restaurants, bars, and hotels in San Francisco served ice in their drinks. Since this was years before the first commercial ice making machine entered the market in 1929, the ice arrived by cargo ship, harvested from Alaska glaciers such as the Mendenhall Glacier in modern day Juneau, Alaska.

*****

It's hard to believe there was a time when people did not demand ice in their drinks.

An American physician named John Gorrie devised a refrigeration plant to help cool the air for his yellow fever patients in 1844, but when he suggested the contraption could be used as an air conditioner, and to manufacture ice for cold drinks, he was practically laughed out of town.

In 1867 Andrew Muhl built an ice making machine to protect meat while in shipment from his San Antonio ranch to nearby Waco. In the decades to follow, the only use for manufactured ice was to preserve food in transit from farms and ranches in the West, to Midwestern and Eastern markets, and not for consumption in chilled drinks.

The commercial production of edible ice took a while to catch on, and it was not until 1929 that Professor Jurgen Hans developed his Kulinda ice machine—just in time for the Great Depression.

*****

What goes better with a cold drink than a bowl of potato chips?

The first potato chip was invented by George Crum in 1853. Crum was an African American chef at a hotel in Saratoga Springs, New York. When a customer complained that the French fries were too soggy, he sliced a potato as thinly as possible, and fried the shaved slices until they were crispy.

A pinch of salt sealed the deal and laid the foundation for one of the world's most popular snack foods. In the United States, over 272 million people claim they eat potato chips either occasionally or regularly. On average, each American consumes 110 pounds of potatoes chips per year, and collectively, 1.5 billion pounds of potatoes are fried into chips annually.

*****

The unique shape of a *Pringle* potato chip has a name. It's called a, hyperbolic paraboloid.

*****

I grew up on what my dad called, *Oklahoma Roll-Ups*. An Oklahoma Roll-Up is a slice of white bread folded over a slice of baloney.

On long trips across the deserts of California, Arizona, and New Mexico, followed by the grassy plains of the Texas Panhandle, my family followed Highway 66 east to Oklahoma several times per year.

We kept it simple, and lived off roll-ups and swigs of water from a canvass water bag everybody carried across the desert in the 1960s.

Not too many years later, I remember my college roommate in Alaska coming home with a story about a sandwich shop, where you could stand in line and pay to have a fast food person make you an Oklahoma Roll-Up.

Of course, they weren't my daddy's roll-ups, but at the time, I simply lacked the imagination to visualize a sandwich as anything but a simple roll-up. My roommate had just experienced a new concept in sandwich fast food…where you hovered over a sneeze guard and side-stepped down the line as you told the sandwich builder exactly how to create your footlong sub sandwich.

But I'm getting ahead of myself. In 2001 I was walking around the campus of Indiana University Pennsylvania in Indiana, Pennsylvania when my stomach told me it was lunch time.

A familiar Denny's sign beckoned from a street next to the school, so I walked that way. En route, I walked past a Subway sandwich shop. A poster of a cold cut trio sandwich, loaded with lettuce, tomatoes, and pickles grabbed my attention. Beside that poster, another poster, featuring a healthy young man holding up a gigantic pair of jeans, sealed the deal.

Sub sandwiches were obviously good for you…and better yet, they didn't look a bit like my dad's Oklahoma Roll-Ups.

*****

The smiling young man in the Subway poster was Jared Fogle. Jared had recently become famous for losing over 200 pounds eating nothing but Subway sandwiches. He was an instant hero and the Subway marketing people used his story to help market their sandwiches as healthy alternatives to burger and fries.

Sadly, in 2015 Jared was charged and convicted of child pornography, and later sentenced to serve 15 years in prison.

Subway wasted no time distancing themselves from the international spokesperson.

*****

Subway is currently the largest fast food chain in the world, in terms of locations, with 44,717 stores...many of which are situate in gas stations, truck stops, and small strip malls.

*****

Subway started humbly, like most American success stories. In 1965, its founder, Fred DeLuca, borrowed $1,000 from his friend, Peter Buck. Fred's idea was to start a sandwich shop to earn money for medical school. By 1978, the franchise operation had spread from coast to coast, with the first West Coast store opening in Fresno, California.

*****

Subway's bestselling sandwich is the BMT. At its conception, the letters "BMT" stood for Brooklyn Manhattan Transit...an obvious tribute to the subway system that services the New York City area. The name was later changed to "Bigger, Meatier, Tastier."

The BMT features Genoa salami, pepperoni, and ham. The sandwich can be customized with the customer's choice of bread style, cheese, and mountains of veggies. While the nutritional value and calories of the BMT varies, depending upon the customer's choice of items and condiments, the basic 6 inch BMT contains 390 calories and 17 grams of fat.

*****

Maize has been a staple food crop in Central America and Mexico for over 4,300 years. Farmers in the region grow over 50 different types of maize, making the crop genetically diverse and resistant to infestation or drought. Maize farmers call the crop varieties landraces, and highly prize their non-GMO food crop.

*****

It's hard to believe, but there are a lot of food and consumer goods that are prohibited from importation into the United States. Obviously, illegal drugs and weapons are banned, but the banned status of some of the food items below may be shocking.

In many cases certain food items are banned based on safety, and the protection of endangered species. But other cases simply reflect our ethnocentricity...that is, our failure to see or want to see the value in food that does not meet our cultural expectations.

Here are ten foods banned in the U.S.:

- Mirabelle Plums grown in France are restricted from importation to the U.S. due to strict French laws regarding the exportation of this fruit.
- Ackee Fruit from Jamaica is prohibited in U.S. due to its ability to cause seizures and dehydration when eaten.
- Queen Conch is a Caribbean sea snail and is prohibited due to over fishing.
- Haggis is a Scottish meal made from sheep liver, hearts, and lungs. Its preparation in the sheep's stomach makes it a big cultural no-no in America.
- Swans are endangered and not allowed for food consumption.
- Pig's Blood Cake from Taiwan is considered unsafe due to suspected unsanitary food handling practices by the importers.
- Wild Beluga Caviar from the Beluga Sturgeon in the Caspian Sea are considered an endangered species.
- The Original Four Loko is a flavored energy drink that contains alcohol.
- Casu Marzu is a Sardinian cheese that traditionally contains live maggots.
- Kinder Surprise Eggs are chocolate covered treats containing a small toy considered a choking hazard.

*****

Sixth grade is an amazing year in a child's life. It's that point where a kid transitions from childhood and elementary school, to middle school and young adulthood.

It's an age of discovery, and a time of self-realization. It's a time when puppy love makes a sudden right turn towards sexual attraction. And it's a time when self-identity and insecurities achieve critical mass.

I learned two things in the sixth grade that stand out from the blur of those halcyon days when my grandmother called me a "spring chick."

First, I discovered the atom bomb, and realized my home's close proximity to a key military installation meant I could be easily vaporized at any second. The sudden realization of one's mortality has a sobering effect on your outlook, and I lost many hours of sleep that year as I watched the night skies from my bedroom window for the tell-tale signs of incoming nuclear tipped rockets.

The second thing I learned was a simple truth—you are what you eat.

About halfway through my sixth grade, the cafeteria lady and the school nurse joined forces to implement their own, pre Michelle Obama, healthy lunch drive.

They made posters with hand drawn fruit and vegetables, and gave each a smiling face. It was supposed to inspire you to want to eat healthy.

They also created a poster depicting a McDonald's Hamburglar type character. They made him look like a desperado who craved burgers and fries above anything else. His fat gut and grumpy scowl was meant to inspire me to avoid fatty foods.

The day I saw that poster was the day I realized I was not one of the pretty people. I was not a cute little fruit. Nor was I a lithe vegetable. I was a slob. A fat loving, burger chomping ne'er-do-well.

I didn't get it at first, but it finally sunk in. I was a product of my diet. And I still am.

Like it or not...I'm the spitting image of the Hamburglar...a little heavy, a little greasy, and a lot of grumpy.

I guess you are what you eat.

The Games People Play

I grew up on the very cusp of the computer revolution. I'm old enough to remember helping my dad replace burned out tubes in our television, and I'm old enough to remember the introduction of personal computers and the transition of games in my local recreation center from pinball and air hockey machines to computerized games like *Pong* and *Donkey Kong*.

Ah, the heady days of my youth, when digital watches were cool, and Jimmy Carter had just returned to peanut farming in Georgia.

Anyway, *Donkey Kong* and *Pong* changed the way we played, and it opened our eyes to the incredible potential of the microchip and personal computing.

Legend has it, when *Donkey Kong* inventor Shigeru Miyamoto created his game in 1981, he stumbled upon the name by accident. Apparently, Shigeru believed the word *donkey* meant *stupid* in English.

His intent was to name the game after the stupid ape portrayed as the main character in the game.

Closer to reality, is the probability Shigeru was mocking the kids who fed quarters into his machines. Perhaps we were the stupid apes Shigeru was thinking of.

*****

If you've ever been to a circus, hired a clown, or stumbled into a street mime, you know about juggling. Jugglers entertain by tossing and catching multiple objects, such as knives, midgets, flaming batons, and bowling pins.

But move over my little Pennywise juggler. The latest trend in juggling is known as *contact juggling*.

In a scene from *The Labyrinth*, the David Bowie character appears to magically move a glass sphere around his hand, transitioning the ball from the top of his hand to his palm with hypnotic ease.

It's not magic. It's actually a beautiful and graceful skill.

*****

The world famous and popular toy manufacturer you may know as *Hasbro*, got its start as a school supply business owned and operated by brothers Henry and Merrill Hassenfeld. The word "Hasbro" is an abbreviation of Hassenfeld Brothers.

*****

Around the time the Hassenfeld brothers shortened their name, a toy inventor named George Lerner from Brooklyn, New York noticed his nephew enjoyed dressing vegetables, such as carrots and potatoes, as humans. Lerner ran with the idea and designed a handful of pushpin eyes, ears, noses, and mouths that could be used to decorate a potato.

In 1949, Lerner tried to market his toy idea, but fell against stiff resistance because it was considered highly wasteful to play with vegetables. In 1952 Lerner approached Hasbro with his product, which came to be known as Mr. Potato Head.

By 1964, the toy had gone completely plastic and was no longer dependent on the use of real vegetables.

Notably, on April 30, 1952, Mr. Potato Head was the first toy to ever be advertised on television, and started a decades long tradition of television advertising by Hasbro. The commercial was also the first time any company had specifically targeted children in its television advertising.

*****

Jackass: The Movie was released in 2002 to an audience of prank loving fans. The movie featured a series of stunts and pranks that invariably involved somebody sustaining a personal injury (or at least the suggestion of an injury). My favorite prank of the movie was the Rent-a-Car Crash-Up Derby, where Johnny Knoxville rents a car and enters it in a Crash Derby.

They then return the destroyed vehicle to the rental agency and contend with the irate agency employee. I'm not sure, but I seem to remember Knoxville had the audacity to ask the rental agency employee for a refund of his fuel deposit.

Personally, I'm not a big fan of prank humor that involves inuring other people. I mean, what's funny about a kid crashing over his bicycle handlebars because a prankster loosened his front wheel? Or, a water skier plowing into a fishing pier?

Not funny.

But pranks, done in good humor and in a loving manner, are hilarious.

I remember getting my car worked on in Bahrain when a person disguised as a representative from the national telephone company (BATELCO) walked up the one lane driveway to the one car garage service center. He was dressed like a technician, wore a hard hat, had rolls of blueprints under one arm, a tool belt around his waist, and a can of red spray paint in his hand.

The man carefully measured the width of the driveway, consulted his blueprints, shrugged his shoulders, and then painted a four inch X in the middle of the driveway.

Curious, the garage owner stopped working on my car, wiped his hands on a grease rag, and approached the so-called technician.

I don't speak Arabic, but I know the conversation went something like this:

"What's this?"

"Location for a new phone booth."

"Phone booth? In my driveway?"

"That's what the work order says. I gotta put a phone booth, right here."

"How am I supposed to get cars in and out of my driveway?"

"Not my problem. Write a letter to BATELCO."

"That'll take weeks."

"Not my problem."

The men went back and forth for several minutes before the garage owner's brother-in-law showed up and revealed the whole thing was a prank. The garage owner stumbled into the garage, found a chair, and nearly passed out. For several minutes he had believed his business and livelihood were going to be screwed over by his own government, and needed several minutes to revive himself before he saw the humor in the prank.

An essential element of a prank like this is the plausibility of truth inherent to the prank. In this case, virtually all governments are notorious bureaucracies, prone to the most stupid behavior...making the possibility a phone booth work order actually existed, and whether the garage owner liked it or not, the phone booth was going in.

Similar gags to this were immortalized on the groundbreaking comedy television show, *Candid Camera*, with Allen Funt. *Candid Camera* first aired on television on August 10, 1948, and lasted 38 seasons.

Here's a handful of harmless pranks you can do at home:

- Tape an aerosol can air horn to the doorstop of your bathroom. When your victim pushes the door open, he or she will be greeted by a sudden, and very loud, blast from the air horn. Don't try this on anybody with a weak heart, or any former soldier suffering from PTSD.
- Television remotes offer an endless supply of prank opportunities. If you own two remotes, you can unobtrusively mess with the volume or channel, leading the viewer to believe his or her television is cracking up. Another option is to cover the light

transmitter portion of the remote with a small piece of electrical tape. When the television viewer attempts to change the channel, the remote won't work.

- Getting people wet when they least expect it is always a hoot. The bucket of water over the door is a classic example of this, but you risk hurting your victim when the bucket invariably falls on his or her head. An alternative way to soak your victim is to place a piece of tape around the nozzle of your kitchen sink faucet. When your victim turns on the water, the water will squirt in their face.

- When it comes to water tricks, the old standby in my childhood home was to flush the toilet while somebody was taking a shower. Due to the water pressure and plumbing in our home, this was guaranteed to jolt the person in the shower with a short blast of hot water. Don't try this if your hot water temperature has the potential to scald or injure your victim.

My mom smoked when I was a child—which may explain the brain damage I now must live with. But on a lighter side, whenever my grandmother came to visit, my mom would hide her cigarettes to avoid a confrontation about her smoking. If my grandmother left the room, my mom would grab a cigarette from its hiding place and dart outside for a quick smoke.

In the interest of having fun, I once removed my mom's cigarette pack from its hiding place and placed the cigarettes in my grandmother's purse. Later that day when my grandmother found the cigarettes she lit into my mom, causing a great deal of anguish.

It seemed fun at the time, but looking back, it was mean. Pure meanness.

I loved it.

*****

Speaking of cigarettes and smoking, smoking is considered the leading cause of preventable deaths in America. Around 480,000 people die each year in the U.S. due to complications related to smoking.

Currently, about 15 percent of adults in America smoke.

*****

To help discourage smoking, and make money from our personal habits, the federal government adds an excise tax of $1.01 to each pack of smokes. Like most states, the state of California adds its own tax to cigarettes, and collects $2.87 per pack. New York has the highest cigarette tax, at $4.35 per pack. Virginia charges the least, at 30 cents per pack—which may or may not be a nod to the tobacco industry in that state.

*****

Based on annual reports and some marketing analysis, it appears Philip Morris spends about 23 to 26 cents to manufacture and package one pack of cigarettes.

Spiders and Snakes, and Everything Great

Friedrich Nietzsche famously wrote in his book, *How to Philosophize with a Hammer*, "that which does not kill me, makes me stronger."

No surprise, as bucolic 19th century Europe was pleasantly immune to earthquakes, hurricanes, tornadoes, and spiders and snakes. Sure, half of Europe succumbed to the Black Death in 1348, but by the time Nietzsche discovered his personal brand of philosophy, the biggest danger to human survival in his neck of the woods was his fellow man.

Because you see, Nietzsche never met a 20 foot Great White shark, or an Australian Funnel Spider.

*****

Jacque Cousteau once stated, "when man enters the water, he enters the food chain. And he is not at the top." And if you've ever encountered a box jellyfish, Cousteau's words may ring especially true.

The box jellyfish makes it home in the warm South Pacific waters around Australia and Indonesia, and is considered the most venomous marine animal in the world. The slightest brush of bare skin against one of their ten foot long tentacles can attack your nervous system, leading to instant pain, heart attack, and death — usually by drowning.

*****

On December 3, 2017, a young woman famous among the Wall Street trader crowd went scuba diving with her friends on a remote island 300 miles off the cost of Costa Rica.

The dive master spotted a tiger shark near the boat. As the divers surfaced he tried and failed to keep the shark off the female victim. Sadly, she died of shock and blood loss before she was able to reach medical help.

Typically, when people think of shark attacks, they think of Great Whites. These behemoths, often in excess of 20 feet in length, can bite a surfer or diver in half without so much as a chipped tooth. In the United States, there are approximately 19 shark attacks annually, with one reported death every two years. Worldwide, over 40 percent of all shark attacks occur in North American waters. Surfers are the most frequent victims of shark attacks with just over half of all attacks. Swimmers and waders account for one third of all shark attacks, with divers actually accounting for only 8 percent of all attacks.

From a shark's perspective, surfers and swimmers look most like a shark's preferred prey — a seal. And in case you didn't know, if you've ever swam or surfed off the coast of Florida, you have been within 10 feet of a shark.

While the odds say you have a 1 out of 3,700,000 chance of dying by shark attack, worldwide, an average of 4 people per year die from shark attack.

Shark attacks are actually rare, compared to the billion other ways you could die. In fact, you are about 10,000 times more likely to be injured in a car accident driving to the beach, than you are of being attacked by a shark. Still, Jacque Cousteau was right. When you enter the water, you enter the food chain.

*****

A whale shark strains over 400,000 gallons of water per hour through its baleen while it is feeding.

*****

The black mamba snake of the eastern and southern regions of the African continent are among the fastest snakes in the world. At over 14 feet in length, an adult black mamba can squirm after you at over 12 miles per hour. When it bites, it delivers enough venom to kill 10 men.

Treatment within 20 minutes is essential for survival. For those unlucky enough to be traveling without a doctor and vial of anti-venom handy, death is nearly 100 percent guaranteed.

*****

Saltwater crocodiles from Southeast Asia down to Australia can grow up to 23 feet in length and weigh over 2,000 pounds. Their strong jaws can exert over 3,700 pounds per square inch of pressure, and account for several hundred deaths per year.

The law of survival with salties is simple…if you don't know what you're doing, stay out of their territory.

*****

Central Africa is home to one of the world's worst insects…the tsetse fly.

About the size of a housefly, the tsetse fly causes the African Sleeping Sickness, which kills approximately 500,000 per year.

*****

The mosquito is the most dangerous critter in the world…in terms of deaths.

There are over 3,000 different types of mosquitos worldwide, and as vectors of diseases like malaria, yellow fever, West Nile virus, and the Zika virus, mosquitos account for over 700,000 deaths each year.

*****

While the deadly creatures discussed above create the most damage to frail humans, nothing conjures fear in the imagination of humans quite like spiders and snakes.

Spiders are like nature's vacuum cleaner. Of the 40,000 spider species known to man, they collectively consume mountains of roaches, flies, earwigs, and other pests. Their venom is also useful in medical research, and synthetic versions of their web silk is being used to design new parachute and bullet-proof vest material.

Yet a handful of spiders dangerous to humans spoils their image. Here are a few spiders worthy of your attention:

- Brazilian Wandering Spider
- Black Widow Spider
- Brown Widow Spider
- Brown Recluse Spider
- Six-Eyed Sand Spider
- Chilean Recluse Spider
- Northern Funnel Web Spider
- Sydney Funnel Web Spider
- Wolf Spider
- Red-Legged Widow Spider

*****

In America, the most common venomous spiders people encounter are black widows and brown recluses.

The brown recluse is by nature, aloof and hard to find. They are about the size of a penny and can move very fast. Recluses are typically found burrowed beneath rocks and debris. They tend to be a gray to light tan color and have a distinctive violin shape on their back — giving the brown recluse the nickname, Fiddle Back.

Its venom destroys skin and muscle tissue, and left untreated can produce a horrific wound.

The black widow spider is the most commonly encountered venomous spider in America. She is glossy black and almost beautiful, in a macabre sense. The tell-tale sign of her widowhood is a bright red hour glass on her abdomen.

Black widows earn their name because they eat their much smaller mates immediately after mating.

Black widows love to hang out in low places, in wood piles, outhouses, and under the eaves of your home. Black widows do not move around much, and spend most of their lives protecting their egg sacks. If you accidentally put your hand in her web, she will attack, giving a painful bite that can result in death.

Death by black widow bite is extremely rare, due to the availability of anti-venom. Historically, most black widow bites occurred in outhouses, where black widows found the ideal nesting area, with plentiful food from flies, and protection from the elements. During the 1950s, 63 people in America died from black widow bites sustained in outhouses.

In 2013, there were 1,866 recorded black widow spider bites. None of those resulted in death. However, the vast majority of black widow bites go unreported, so this actual number may be much higher.

*****

In the world of snakes, is it any wonder that Saint Patrick banished all the snakes from Ireland. Outside of Ireland, keep your eyes open for these squirmy guys, rated among the top most venomous snakes in the world:

- Belcher's Sea Snake
- Eastern Brown Snake
- Blue Krait
- Taipan
- Black Mamba
- Tiger Snake
- Philippine Cobra
- Saw Scaled Viper
- Death Adder
- Rattlesnake

*****

The Taipan snake from Australia can kill up to 12,000 guinea pigs with one bite. Without treatment, a human victim will die within one hour. Prior to the development of an anti-venom, bites from this snake were 100 percent fatal.

*****

One of the most interesting, and potentially deadly, snakes in America is the Mojave Green. This snake is a small pit viper, related to the rattlesnake. It makes its home in the Desert Southwest, particularly in the High Desert region of Southern California and parts of Northern Mexico.

What makes this snake interesting is its venom, which has characteristics of both the rattlesnake and water moccasin venoms. This means its bite serves a lethal injection of both neurotoxic (nerve) and hemotoxic (blood) venom — making it the most toxic rattlesnake in the world, and about 16 times more powerful than a sidewinder's venom.

*****

Outside of Alaska and Hawaii, the United States plays host to over 20 species of venomous snakes. Most of these snakes are from the rattlesnake family, with two different types of coral snake, one species of cottonmouth or water moccasin, and one species of copperhead.

Health officials estimate approximately 8,000 people are bitten by venomous snakes in the U.S. annually, with five of those bites leading to death. Ironically, while the Mojave Green rattlesnake is rated the most toxic among rattlers, the Eastern and Western Diamondback rattlers cause the most fatalities.

*****

Technically speaking, snakes do not like Ireland. While the lack of snakes is attributed to St Patrick voting them off the island, in fact, snakes never lived in Ireland to begin with.

*****

Here's a double handful of phobias your mother may not have taught you:

- Acrophobia: Fear of heights
- Arachnophobia: Fear of spiders
- Ophidiophobia: Fear of snakes
- Agoraphobia: Fear of panic attacks
- Mysophobia: Fear of germs
- Cynophobia: Fear of dogs
- Androphobia: Fear of men
- Bibliophobia: Fear of books
- Cacophobia: Fear of ugliness
- Coprastasophobia: Fear of constipation
- Eurotophobia: Fear of female genitalia
- Sesquipedalophobia: Fear of long words
- Ambulophobia: Fear of walking (My personal favorite)

*****

In the realm of phobias, you may be shocked to learn there is an actual scientific condition known as *boanthropy*. If you suffer from this condition, you believe you are a cow.

But what if you think you have been reincarnated as a rat?

*****

In Rajasthan, India, the Karni Mata Temple is a refuge for over 20,000 rats.

But these aren't ordinary, run-of-the-mill rats. No. These rats are the reincarnated souls of descendants of the Hindu Goddess, Karni Mata.

Apparently, the Goddess pleaded with Yoma, the Hindu God of Death, for the life of her drowned son. He agreed, with one proviso. Her son and all the male descendants of her family would come back as rats.

Visitors to the temple feed the rats, and carefully avoid stepping on them as they admire the furry rodents. Worshippers also believe it is good luck to eat portions of the food set out for the rats.

Most of us would cringe at the thought of visiting a rat-infested building, and even fewer would consider eating leftovers from a rat's feast. But faith is faith, and who am I to question what another person believes?

*****

Snails are the scourge of every garden, and it's not uncommon to find devoted gardeners using a flashlight and bucket to collect and destroy the slow crawlers.

The collective noun for snails is a *rout*. Which also works to describe my plans last spring. In the process of researching how to rout out the snails in my garden I was shocked to learn snails have 14,000 teeth, and some can even kill you. No thanks. I guess I'll be sending the wife out with a bucket and flashlight to save my garden.

While many species of snail can be eaten, roasted in a bath of garlic butter, there are poisonous snails. In fact, the cone snail is considered one of the most toxic animals on the planet, and uses a harpoon like stinger to kill its prey.

The cone snail hangs out in the ocean waters off the coast of Southern California and 65 percent of its human victims die. Ironically, the venom from a cone snail is a powerful painkiller, considered 1,000 times more potent than morphine.

*****

To Nietzsche's credit, his quote about gaining strength from that which does not kill him may have pertained more to a man's character or his judgment than his ability to survive an accident or tragic event. Interestingly, Nietzsche strived to understand how humans respond to environmental stimulus, and how this response may be elevated to improve an individual's ability to think and reason.

Character flaws and rash behaviors, in short, were the result of an individual's inability to NOT respond to stimulus.

For example, if you are a caught in the bed of another man's wife (the stimulus), the affronted husband's response may be deemed rash, violent, or even illegal. In another example, if a driver cuts in front of you on the highway (the stimulus), your response may be to lean on the horn, throw him the finger, ram him, or even follow him home so you can verbally assault him in front of his friends and family and earn yourself a well-deserved restraining order.

Nietzsche saw these stimulus-response scenarios as opportunities for mankind to rise above instinctive or animalistic responses; therefore, making the individual stronger and more capable of defusing the next stimulus-response situation.

That said, if you ever catch an unwelcome guest in your bed…well…Nietzsche be damned.

Oh, the Humanity

In the early days of commercial aviation, and the rising popularity of traveling by air, many people believed the safest and most comfortable way to fly was via dirigible.

This dream of floating over land and sea in 5-star hotel type luxury came to an explosive end on May 6, 1937 when the German airship, Hindenburg, exploded as it approached its landing site at Lakehurst Airfield in New Jersey.

Analysis of the crash video by NASA (years after the event), suggests the total elapsed time from the first indication of flames erupting from the hull of the ship to its bow cascading to the ground in ruins lasted only 16 seconds. Passengers and crew had mere seconds to make life or death decisions to jump and run, or ride the ship down and hope for the best.

35 people died in the fiery crash: 13 passengers and 22 crew members.

Radio commentator Herbert Morrison, working for a Chicago based radio station, recorded the event and is remembered for his heartfelt and dramatic description of the tragedy, immortalizing the phrase, "Oh, the humanity."

*****

In the course of human events, the Hindenburg was a massive tragedy for the time. Morrison watched in slow motion as 35 people perished in flames, and it's no wonder he called it the "worst of the world's worst catastrophes.". But the Hindenburg tragedy hardly rises to the level of human suffering experienced in air travel since.

To date, the worst air disaster in history didn't happen in the air, but on the ground.

On a foggy afternoon on the Canary Islands, located off the western coast of North Africa, 583 passengers and crew died in a ground collision between two Boeing 747 passenger jets.

Pan Am flight 1736 had been instructed by the control tower to taxi in preparation for take-off.

Simultaneously, KLM Flight 4805 had received what it interpreted as permission to take-off.

The aircraft collided on the runway, killing all aboard the KLM flight. 61 passengers and crew members aboard the Pan Am flight survived.

Gross incompetence, weather, and miscommunication were all contributing factors in the accident.

And this is exactly how accidents happen. Usually, a single mistake is survivable, but where two or more mistakes occur simultaneously, people die.

For example, a child and his mother recently died in a traffic accident near my home. Apparently, the father pulled his vehicle into the emergency lane of the freeway due to a flat tire. He was less than 100 yards away from an exit off-ramp. Immediately after stopping his vehicle, a drunk driver collided into the back of his vehicle.

The father did nothing legally wrong by stopping in the emergency lane. However, considering the risks of stopping on the freeway, with cars traveling 70 miles per hour mere inches from your doorknob, not limping forward to the exit ramp may have been a mistake.

In the best of circumstances, stopping on the freeway to change a tire rates as an inconvenience. But when you combine this with the arrival of a drunk driver, you have all the ingredients for a disaster.

This "intersection" of mistakes and incidents is also apparent in the Canary Islands disaster:

- A terrorist threat earlier in the day caused the main airport on the island to close down. All traffic was diverted to the secondary airport at Tenerife.
- Tenerife was essentially fogged in, making visibility very poor.
- The KLM pilots assumed they had been given clearance to take-off.
- Rather than order a full stop to ground operations, air traffic controllers presumably accepted the lack of being able to see two Boeing 747 passenger jets facing off on the same runway as an acceptable risk.

*****

Naming your baby is important. And it's something to take seriously. Faddish names, obscene names, and names that promulgate your political opinions, can be deadly to your child's future.

For example, a couple in New Jersey, who are obviously sympathetic to Nazism and Hitler, named their son, Adolf Hitler. Perhaps even worse, some parents give their children obscene names, like Nipple Twister, and Hard One.

America is one of the only countries in the world that allow parents near carte blanche when it comes to naming their child. And why not? We take pride in our civil liberties. But some parents can't handle this awesome responsibility.

Here are just a few of the weird names parents have used to complete their new baby's birth certificate:

- Hellzel
- Abcde
- Orgasm
- Panty
- M'y'ai-un-a

The last name on this list reminds me of a joke about a girl named, La-uh.

Apparently, the mother visited the school to complain that her daughter's teacher repeatedly mispronounced her daughter's name, calling her, Lauh. When the principal asked for the correct pronunciation, the mother responded, "It's La Dash Ah. The dash don't be silent."

As one of my more profane military commanders once said, "there's no defense against ignorance."

*****

Sociologists have found the name you give a child influences who they become, their job prospects, and even other people's perception of their trustworthiness. If your child's future matters to you, set aside your ego for a minute and find a popular or common name.

Here are the top five boy's names in 2017:

- Noah
- Liam
- Mason

- Jacob
- William

Here are the top five girl's names in 2017:

- Emma
- Olivia
- Sophia
- Ava
- Isabella

No hyphens. No misspellings. And no obscenities. No illiterate letter and punctuation machinations. Just solid names that will serve your child well, for life.

*****

It's a simple fact of life and nature…men spend over one year of their life staring at women. If you add the 120 minutes per week men spend watching porn on the Internet, you can surmise the instinct to notice and lust for the opposite sex remains strong in the age of soy boys and feminism.

*****

And when a man's lust is not properly satiated, he can turn to violence. Half of the female homicide victims in America were murdered by current or former partners. And to get away with it, men resort to lying…a skill they have honed from a lifetime of lying 6 times more often than their female counterparts.

*****

But karma has a way of coming back at you, as men are five times more likely than women to be struck by lightning, and routinely die 3 to 7 years earlier than women. Incidentally, male teenagers are three times more likely to die due to reckless or violent behavior than women the same age.

*****

The New Testament *Book of James* reminds us that, "the fervent prayer of a righteous man availeth much." During the Middle Ages, entire monasteries and convents were built and supported to facilitate fervent prayer.

The way the feudal lords and peasants of the time saw things, the prayer of the faithful gave them the leeway to pursue their terrestrial life, without the inconvenience of constant supplication. In those days, the firstborn male in a family was predestined to inherit the family estate and business. The second son was expected to join the church. And the rest of the sons automatically trained for the military. As for daughters, if they were not to be strategically wed, they were better off joining a convent and quietly going away.

The feudal system was great for church recruitment, but for many, their involvement in the church was not the result of true fervor or an undying urge to serve the Church...except for the anchorites.

An anchorite was typically female, but could be male. They were the nun's nun, and the monk's monk. They wanted nothing but to be left alone in silence to pray and meditate. To accommodate their fervor, monasteries and convents built small huts in the woods where the anchorite could live in isolation.

An anchorite hut did not even have a door. Food and water was provided through a food slot, much like the food slots in a maximum security prison cell. An anchorite's sole purpose in life was to pray for the salvation of mankind.

So, if a hermit's life seems like your way out of the rat race, you may want to consider becoming an anchorite. It's not for everybody, and an anchorite's life ain't easy.

But neither is pimping.

*****

The major faiths or religions of the world include:

- Christianity (2.1 billion)
- Islam (1.3 billion)
- Hinduism (900 million)
- Chinese traditional religion (394 million)
- Buddhism 376 million

Just over 1 billion people identify as either agnostic, atheist, or non-religious.

*****

Despite evidence to the contrary, marriage is seen as one of the biggest factors in determining happiness and economic stability among adults. In America, ten cities stood out from the rest as marriage hotspots, with marriage rates ranging from 45-50 percent of adults:

- Dallas, Texas
- Charlotte, North Carolina
- San Diego, California
- Houston, Texas
- El Paso, Texas
- Phoenix, Arizona
- San Antonio, Texas
- San Jose, California
- Fort Worth, Texas
- Jacksonville, Florida

I suppose if you're looking to get married, or want to start a wedding service type business, head to Texas!

*****

Cities with highest divorce rates in America include:

- Detroit, Michigan
- Rochester, New York
- Cleveland, Ohio
- Miami, Florida
- Newark, New Jersey

Interestingly, Detroit also rates as the unhappiest city in America…which is what happens when manufacturing jobs disappear and women suddenly find themselves tripping over their unemployed husbands all day.

*****

Cities with the lowest divorce rates in America include:

- Plano, Texas
- Overland Park, Kansas
- Gilbert, Arizona
- Irvine, California
- Santa Clarita, California

I have no idea what they add to the water in these communities, but I suspect the low divorce rates may have something to do with the popularity of his and hers separate bathrooms in these areas…but I'm just guessing.

Crime and Punishment

School districts and the careers of school principals hang on the success and failure of their respective students, and while school officials are quick to point to graduation rates and test scores as indicators of their success as educators, a more revealing indicator of their failure is the so-called functional illiteracy of their graduates.

Functional illiteracy is defined as the inability to read and comprehend information critical to daily life management. For example, being unable to accurately read or comprehend the dosage instructions on a prescription medication bottle poses obvious risks.

In a less deadly example of how functional illiteracy impacts lives, consider the advertisements you receive in the mail daily.

My local cable company routinely sends out flyers announcing incredible rates for television, phone, and Internet connectivity. The small print reveals the amazing rate is not in fact for the entire package, but the rate for each element of the package. So, when the bold print announces phone, television, and Internet for only $29,95, the real price is closer to $90. Further small print reveals this rate is only available with a two-year contract.

But a functionally illiterate person would never see beyond the bold red print announcing a great deal.

Functional illiteracy drives people to spend money foolishly, commit crimes, miss opportunities, and lead lives of quiet desperation. Consider these sad numbers:

- Within the walls of our infamous prison system, 60 percent of all inmates cannot read above the 4th grade level.
- In our juvenile correction system, 8 out of 10 juvenile inmates are considered functionally illiterate.
- In economic terms, functional illiteracy accounts for over 40 percent of the people who live below the poverty line.
- Over 65 percent of students who cannot read at grade level by the 4th grade will go on to lead a life of crime and spend time in the prison system.
- 75 percent of the people on food stamps are either illiterate, or functionally illiterate.
- Teenage girls who cannot read at their grade level are 6 times more likely to become pregnant than their literate peers.

Wow!

Illiteracy sucks.

*****

Speaking of prisons, the United States, known worldwide as the land of the free, incarcerates one quarter of the world's 10 million prisoners.

Unlike soft-hearted places like Sweden or Finland who tend to counsel and rehabilitate criminals rather than imprison them, and places like Saudi Arabia that simply execute you by next Thursday, the United States prefers to house its criminals in long term holding pens, like cattle in a feedlot.

*****

Delving beneath the surface numbers, it's interesting to see how our prison population is divided among the races.

- 39 percent of prisoners are White, while Whites comprise 69 percent of the U.S. population.
- 19 percent of prisoners are Hispanic, while Hispanics comprise 16 percent of the U.S. population.
- 40 percent of prisoners are Black, while Blacks comprise 13 percent of the U.S. population.

In raw numbers, 450 out of every 100,000 Whites in America are imprisoned, while 831 out of 100,000 are Hispanic, and 2,306 out of 100,000 are Black.

*****

So, what's an average guy gotta do in America to earn three hots and a cot in Uncle Sam's housing project?

If you live in Ferguson, Missouri, failure to pay your traffic tickets can land you in jail, and failure to pay your court mandated child support — whether you have a job or not — can earn you a ticket to the farm in virtually every jurisdiction within the United States.

But in most cases, the inmate population is made up of drug traffickers, armed robbers, rapists, and murderers.

Engineering a Brave New World

Americans are in love with their disposable lifestyle. I'm not saying it's a good thing, or a bad thing. It just is.

The problem, according to the Environmental Protection Agency (EPA), who has its own history of lousy and politically motivated practices and policies, is how we choose to dispose of our waste.

While it doesn't sound like much, Americans create 4 pounds of trash each, every day. That adds up to over 250 million tons of trash each year. We create more trash than any other nation on Earth, and only manage to recycle about 34 percent of it.

Nationwide, there are approximately 10,000 officially designated municipal waste facilities.

But if you've ever paid attention to the debris dumped in alleys and along country roads, you'd know the actual number of dumpsites is astronomical.

Most of the solutions to this problem seem to focus on reducing the creation of trash at the consumer level.

For example, in California a ban on disposable plastic bags used to carry out your groceries has created a huge tote bag industry, while significantly reducing the number of plastic bags that used to blanket city streets and clog storm drains.

But this change came with a lot of pain. Because you see, consumers love their packaging.

Perhaps an easier way to deal with the trash problem is not to attempt to change people's consumption habits, but to improve the economic and environmental viability of recyclables. That is, make it easier to recycle, and make more disposable products recyclable.

Trust me. If you make it worthwhile to recycle a product, there's a man with a shopping cart and a seemingly endless supply of leaf size trash bags, ready to pick it up.

*****

Bombshell silver screen actress Hedy Lamarr was famous for a lot of things, including a nude scene in the 1933 movie *Ecstasy*, where she simulated an orgasm and earned the condemnation of both the Pope and Adolf Hitler.

After leaving her home in Vienna and hooking up with Louis Mayer from MGM fame, she began to build an acting career in Hollywood. She quickly adapted to her adopted home of America and fell in with the likes of Howard Hughes, where her genius for engineering and inventing came to fruition.

During World War II, Hedy worked tirelessly to invent things for the Allied war effort, including a secure communication system that came to be known as *frequency hopping*--used by the U.S. military to this day.

*****

The theoretical physicist Stephen Hawking has publicly stated many times that humans should keep quiet, and not alert the Universe to our presence. According to him, if aliens do exist and have the ability to travel to Earth, then by definition they would be more advanced than us, and pose an extinction level threat to humanity. He is also outspoken about the dangers of artificial intelligence, and the use of robots.

Hawking is not anti-technology or anti-development. But he does not trust the developers of artificial intelligence and robots to do the right thing.

Perhaps his opinions are being shaped by science fiction, where the slight tweaking of a robot or computer's programming transforms a servant of humanity into a killer.

Isaac Asimov captured that sentiment in his classic story, *I, Robot*, where a mainframe computer outgrew her creator's programming and built herself an army of human killing robots.

Arthur C. Clarke also portrayed a mainframe computer going off track with his classic, *2001: A Space Odyssey*. And decades after Asimov and Clarke laid the foundation for errant technology, Arnold Schwarzenegger portrayed a human hating robot in *Terminator*.

Every one of these science fiction stories focus on the bad programming of a computer or robot. Is it any wonder Hawking is nervous about the future? Think about it. We live in a world where computers are hacked almost daily. Why would the hacking of a robot be out of the realm of reality?

In recent history, hackers, who think of themselves as social engineers or modern day Robin Hoods, have used the weak link in computers (the human programmers and operators) to uncover government secrets, rob banks, kidnap databases, and monitor your keyboard strokes.

*****

In 1988, a graduate student at Cornell University named Robert Morris created the first worm virus to infiltrate the backbone of the Internet in its infancy.

Morris subsequently earned another 15 minutes of fame when he became the first person to earn a conviction under the Computer Fraud and Abuse Act. He was sentenced to 400 hours of community service and fined $10,050. We can only hope the court did not assign him to perform his community service in the local bank, or the courthouse computer room.

His actions, while deemed somewhat innocent of malignant intent, laid the foundation for destructive and expensive hacks to come.

*****

In one of the first hacks motivated by money, Russian hacker Valdimir Levin stole $3.7 million from Citibank in 1995.

Exploiting the human weakness link, Vladimir managed to steal passwords to bank accounts, and used these passwords to access accounts and transfer money. Vladimir operated out of London, but somehow managed to get tangled up with the FBI and was arrested. He served 3 years in prison, and was ordered to repay $210,000 to Citibank.

Let's see…three years in prison for $3.7 million? Who said crime does not pay?

*****

In 1999 a 16 year old named Jonathan James hacked into the International Space Station and played games with the station's environmental control system.

No biggie, right? Astronauts don't need oxygen or heat in space.

Fortunately, the space station was not equipped with a laser gun. The temptation to zap a city or two may have been too tantalizing.

*****

In October 2016, a hacker cracked the Uber (the private taxi service company that manages to operate without taxicabs, or commercially licensed drivers) database, accessing over 57 million consumer accounts.

Uber apparently hid the data breach from the public, and paid the hackers $100,000 to delete the stolen data. Apparently, the hackers were able to access the Uber database via an account on the Amazon Web Services site.

Web services is another word for cloud service, where large organizations like Amazon sell data storage space on their computer servers.

Cloud services are becoming more and more popular in the computer industry, suggesting future hacks could be even more devastating if and when hackers gain access to massive centrally stored files.

*****

Beyond the imaginary world of science fiction writers and the all too real actions of computer hackers, automation and the rise of robotics is impacting lives, as we speak (read).

I grew up in a mining town, and for nearly 50 years the mining company was the primary employer of around 1,200 employees. In 1981 this all changed when automation allowed the company to lay off many of its laborers, employed in various jobs that involved monitoring gauges, turning valves, and handling material.

Within a handful of years, my childhood hometown was transformed from a vibrant and exciting place to live, to a virtual ghost town. My parents did not foresee the change, and my dad fell victim to one of the first waves of layoffs.

Automation is coming to a town near you, and it's going to change the way you live and work.

The food service and hotel industries employ over 13.7 million Americans, and experts estimate up to 54 percent of the jobs in these industries an be automated, using today's technology.

This change is evident where fast food outlets like McDonald's have already deployed kiosks to train customers to place their own orders.

Behind the front counter, in what McDonald's calls the "back of the house," technology already exists to automate the production of fried foods, and to even manufacture hamburgers.

The final transformation to a virtually non-human fast food restaurant is just a matter of time as customers adapt to the change, and corporate officers commit to the dramatic cultural changes.

In the hotel industry, automated vacuum cleaners clean long hallways and lobby floors, and automated window cleaners move up and down the exterior of buildings, without fear of heights. In the front lobby, kiosks, similar to those used at airports, allow guests to check-in and claim their room keys (smart cards), without human intervention.

Again, it's just a matter of training consumers to accept robotic hospitality, over the human touch.

In New York, Amazon is testing a small grocery outlet that operates like a giant, walk-in vending machine. Customers select food products, and as they place the food in their cart, the so-called "Internet of Everything" recognizes the movement of the food item and automatically charges you for it. When you're finished shopping, you can carry your food to the sidewalk and hop into an autonomous driven Uber vehicle.

*****

The technology used by Amazon in its self-serve grocery store is based on RFID technology. RFID stands for Radio Frequency Identification, and it is an essential part of what makes the chip in car key fob and your credit cards, work.

RFID technology uses scanners to constantly seek, find, and read the information on RFID chips within its range. If you have a credit card or debit card with a chip embedded in it, RFID scanners can read it. As you walk down the street, hundreds of RFID readers are recognizing and reading your banking data.

This does not mean the RFID readers can initiate an unauthorized purchase, but they do have access to your personal and banking information. RFID scanners are readily available in the market, and it's only a matter of time before massive heists via RFID encryption exploitation becomes a reality.

Lethal Stupidity and the Prized Darwin Awards

There's one award in America you do not want.

They call it the Darwin Award, in reference to Charles Darwin and his theory of the survival of the fittest.

To win this award, you have to die a gruesome and totally avoidable manner. Bonus points are awarded based on the victim's blood alcohol content at the time of the fatal incident, and extra bonus points are given if the event is recorded or witnessed by the victim's buddies.

Darwin Awards are almost exclusively given to men, aged 18-25, as women are generally less inclined to engage in testosterone and alcohol induced acts of stupidity.

Women are also under represented here because, by definition, they do not suffer from what trauma center doctors call young buck syndrome. That is, the tendency to see oneself as superhuman, immortal, and immune to pain or injury.

*****

Bungee jumping is inherently dangerous…which is why it's so much fun.

All you have to do is tie yourself to a rope, secure the other end of the rope to a bridge or other sturdy object spanning the open space you wish to jump from, and then toss yourself into the abyss.

Don't worry, the abyss you are jumping into does not care that you exist and is not staring back at you. Done properly, the rope tied to your ankles will stop you before you hit the ground.

Sadly, as a young man from West Virginia discovered, tying the rope around your ankles is not enough. You also have to make sure the other end of the rope is secured to the bridge.

The drop was only 70 feet, but anything over 50 feet is almost always fatal. In Canada, emergency responders have found any fall of over 16 feet can lead to death.

But you don't have to go rock climbing, sky diving, bungee jumping, or tree climbing to suffer a fatal fall. Over 500,000 people die each year from slip and fall accidents…which is basically the same as falling from zero feet high.

*****

In 2008, Brazilian priest Adelir Antônio de Carli built himself a cluster balloon by tying 1,000 helium balloons to a lawn chair. The priest bravely took a seat, released the ground tether, and instantly ascended to 19,700 feet before disappearing.

Pieces of his cluster balloon and his body were later found at sea.

*****

In 1997 a Pennsylvania man was playing with his friend's pet cobra when the snake did exactly what millions of years of evolution dictated — it bit him.

The man apparently refused medical care, claiming, "I'm a man. I can take it."

The two men then went to a local tavern to share their story of manliness, where the snakebite victim promptly died. Rumor has it he was not able to finish his beer and was charged, post mortem, for alcohol abuse.

*****

In 2011, a New York motorcycle enthusiast was participating in a helmet law protest ride. Riding without a helmet, he crashed during the ride and died of a head injury.

*****

In South Korea a wheelchair bound man rammed his wheelchair against an elevator door after the elevator door closed before he could enter the elevator.

Somehow, ramming the elevator door caused the door to open, allowing the man to plunge down the elevator shaft to his death.

*****

The people who determine whether a person's death or serious injury warrants inclusion in the Darwin Award roster of lethal stupidity, judges assess nominations using the following criteria:

- Veracity (the event is verifiable)
- Excellence (act showed incredible stupidity)
- Inability to Reproduce (victim must be dead or unable to reproduce)
- Maturity (victim must be an adult and capable of normal sound judgment)
- Self Selection (victim's actions led to his own death or injury)

*****

Beyond the tragic and totally avoidable, most of us die of natural causes, disease, and accidents. Among those accident statistics are the sad stories of motorcycle enthusiasts, who are 26 times more likely to die in a traffic accident than the occupants of four wheeled vehicles.

While the inherent danger of riding on two wheels among a world of four-wheelers is obvious, what about riding on one wheel?

In my hometown there is a restaurant popular with motorcycle people. I'm not talking about Harley's, favored by older men. No. I'm talking about the rice rockets, capable of doing 150 miles per hour in a quarter mile. In short, I'm talking about riders between the ages of 18 and 29.

The restaurant features an outdoor patio dining area that faces onto a four-lane highway. On Friday nights it is not uncommon to see a hundred or more motorcycles in the parking lot, with dozens of motorcycles coming and going on the highway.

One Friday night an intrepid rider grabbed his girlfriend and proceeded to do a wheelie down the four-lane highway as he left the restaurant. Within seconds he was doing over 100 miles per hour, on his back wheel. How his girlfriend managed to hang on is beyond me, but together they plowed into a light pole less than two hundred yards from the restaurant.

Stunts like this are what gives motorcycles a bad name. Sure, motorcycles are built for fun — and they are — but they also enable stupidity.

According to the U.S. National Highway Traffic Safety Administration (NHTSA), an average of 13 cars out of every 100,000 end up being involved in a fatal crash each year. For motorcycles, the average is 72 for every 100,000 motorcycles.

In 2015, 4,693 motorcyclists died in accidents. While getting tangled up with a four-wheel vehicle is often blamed as the cause for these fatal crashes, 41 percent of motorcycle fatalities did not involve another vehicle.

In 1975, 80 percent of motorcycle fatalities involved a rider under the age of 30. Thankfully, this percentage has dropped dramatically to 30 percent. Over the course of the same years, fatalities for riders over 50 years old have gone from 3 percent of all riders, to over 35 percent of all riders.

*****

Make no mistake, motorcycle riders do not hold a monopoly on dying on what the Ohio State Highway Patrol calls the *Red Asphalt*.

Air bags and the increased use of seatbelts have saved countless lives, but traffic fatalities are on the rise, with 94 percent of all fatalities attributable to what the National Highway Traffic Safety Administration calls "human choices" — that is, speeding, or driving while intoxicated.

In 2016, 37,461 people died in traffic accidents. Worldwide, approximately 1.2 million people die each year in traffic accidents.

*****

Outside of illnesses, cancers, and other health related fatalities, the top five causes of death, according to the World Health Organization are:

- Vehicle related traffic accidents
- Self-inflicted injuries
- Interpersonal violence
- Drowning
- War and conflicts

*****

In the United States, 31,959 people died from unintentional falls in 2014. That same year, 42,032 Americans died from unintentional poisoning. In 2013, 42,826 Americans committed suicide, with 50 percent of those by firearm.

*****

74 percent of all deaths in America can be attributed to the top 10 causes of death, presented below in rank order:

- Heart disease
- Cancer
- **CHRONIC** bronchitis and emphysema
- Accidents
- Stroke
- Alzheimer's disease
- Diabetes

- Influenza and pneumonia
- Kidney failure
- Suicide

Late Night Thoughts on Literature, YouTube, and Harry Potter

Long before I gave up the tourist game, I took an obligatory trip to London to see what all the fuss was about. After a day of perusing the typical hangouts, my wife and I got lost walking back to our bed and breakfast. After an hour of stumbling in the dark we followed a light towards the only sign of life in the neighborhood — a pub.

We walked into the loud pub and into the middle of a game of pub trivia. Trust me, the English are serious about their pub trivia.

The first question we heard asked the competitors to identify Romeo's last name from the tragic play *Romeo and Juliet* by Shakespeare. My wife knew the answer and nearly shouted out Montague.

None of the players correctly answered the question.

As it turns out, movie and literature questions are popular categories in the pub trivia circuit. So, in the interest of helping make the world a better place for people interested in showing off in pub trivia contests, here's a little knowledge for you.

*****

Shakespeare's plays in alphabetical order, followed by the year each play was believed to have been written, include:

- All's Well That Ends Well (1602)
- Antony and Cleopatra (1606)
- As You Like It (1599)
- Comedy of Errors (1589)
- Coriolanus (1607)
- Cymbeline (1609)
- Hamlet (1600)
- Henry IV, Part I (1597)
- Henry IV, Part II (1597)
- Henry V (1598)
- Henry VI, Part I (1591)
- Henry VI, Part II (1590)
- Henry VI, Part III (1590)
- Henry VIII (1612)
- Julius Caesar (1599)
- King John (1596)
- King Lear (1605)
- Love's Labor's Lost (1594)
- Macbeth (1605)
- Measure for Measure (1604)

- Merchant of Venice (1596)
- Merry Wives of Windsor (1600)
- Midsummer Night's Dream (1595)
- Much Ado about Nothing (1598)
- Othello (1604)
- Pericles (1608)
- Richard II (1595)
- Richard III (1592)
- Romeo and Juliet (1594)
- Taming of the Shrew (1593)
- Tempest (1611)
- Timon of Athens (1607)
- Titus Andronicus (1593)
- Troilus and Cressida (1601)
- Twelfth Night (1599)
- Two Gentlemen of Verona (1594)
- Winter's Tale (1610)

Wow! I can only describe the plot or storyline of about five of the plays listed above...then again, I tend to exaggerate my sweet skills.

*****

Speaking of sweet skills, what is the name of the actor who portrayed Napoleon in the movie *Napoleon Dynamite*? I'll give you a minute to think about it while I Google the correct answer.

There it is. Sweet. Napoleon was played by Jon Heder, who is also known for a more serious role as Walt Disney's brother Roy, in the movie, *Walt Before Mickey*.

While Walt was obviously the genius behind the Walt Disney empire, his brother Roy played a critical role in managing Walt's studio, and later became recognized as one of the most influential CEOs in American business.

*****

Did you know park employees at Disneyland are trained to point using both their index and middle fingers together? This two-fingered style of pointing is believed to be a tribute to Walt, who always pointed using two fingers. What people tend to forget is that Walt was a chain smoker, and almost always had a cigarette between his index and middle fingers.

His two-fingered point was the only way he could point out attractions in his park to guests without dropping his cigarette.

*****

Now, I'm not a big fan of cigarettes, and I certainly don't miss the fog of cigarette smoke that inevitably found its way into your lungs wherever two or more gathered. But sometimes I get nostalgic for the old cigarette commercial marketing jingles.

You may be too young to remember, but there was a time when the biggest name shows and sporting events on television paid their bills and pocketed their profits on the backs of cigarette sawbucks.

Cigarette commercials were banned from television and radio in 1971 following the enactment of the Public Health Cigarette Smoking Act. The last cigarette commercial aired on the Johnny Carson Show on January 1, 1971.

Here are a handful of addicting cigarette jingles:

- Winston tastes good, like a cigarette should.
- I'd walk a mile for a Camel.
- You can take Salem out of the country, but you can't take the country out of Salem.
- You've come a long way, baby (Virginia Slims).
- Lady be Kool.
- We'd rather fight than switch (Tareyton).

And my personal favorite, the image of a cowboy riding his horse to the theme song for *The Magnificent Seven* used by Marlboro

*****

Marlboro has been the most popular cigarette around the world for decades. The cigarette makers originally targeted an upper-class market, using the name Marlboro to denote some kind of F. Scott Fitzgerald, *The Great Gatsby*, image. It failed. When the cigarette marketers shifted their brand imagery to a lone cowboy, presumably riding the fences like the desperado in the hit song *Desperado* by the Eagles, demand surged.

Years later, TWA Flight 847 from Athens to Rome was hijacked on June 14, 1985. During the siege a Navy diver named Robert Stethem was shot and tossed from the airplane in a brutal and haunting display of desperation by the terrorists. Following a two-week hostage stand-off in Beirut, the Hezbollah terrorists released most of the hostages. Five of the passengers were singled out and removed to hide-outs in Lebanon, and later released.

Following the ordeal, passengers remembered the terrorists wanting to visit America so they could meet J.R. Ewing from the television show, *Dallas*, and the Marlboro Man.

The terrorist ringleader, Mohammed Ali Hamadei, was later captured in Germany and spent 19 years in prison. While unconfirmed, it is believed he died in a CIA drone attack in Pakistan in 2010.

But I digress.

*****

Did you know Taylor Swift's video, *Blank Space*, has over 2.2 billion views? It was originally posted to YouTube on November 10, 2014. The video has over 514,000 comments and 7 million Thumbs Up. 600K viewers gave the video a Thumbs Down.

While I'm not a big fan of Taylor Swift, I at least know her name and know she sings, right? But as of December 2017, the most viewed video on YouTube is called *Despacito* by some guy named Luis Fonsi, with 4.4 billion views.

Who's Fonsi? Wasn't he the leather clad gangster motorcycle guy from *Happy Days*? And what about all those silly kitten videos? I thought they were the top viewed videos online.

By the way, the Fonz from *Happy Days* was played by Henry Winkler.

*****

YouTube first entered the online scene on February 14, 2005. It was the creation of a group of Paypal employees, Chad Hurley, Steve Chen, and Jawed Karim, who wanted a place online to share home videos with each other.

Jawed Karim posted the first video to YouTube on April 23, 2005. It was called, *Me at the Zoo*.

Here are some awesome facts about YouTube you just gotta know:

- YouTube claims to have approximately 1.3 billion registered users.
- Every minute of every day, users upload over 300 hours of new video material to the site.
- 30 million daily visitors watch over 5 billion videos each day, making it the second busiest website online, after its parent, Google.
- Men tend to prefer YouTube over women, with 62 percent of all views coming from men.
- 35-44 year old men comprise the largest single group of visitors.

- YouTube supports titles, descriptions, and keywords in 76 different languages.
- People are fickle about their videos, with a significant portion of those viewers watching only the first 10 seconds of any given video.
- Google purchased YouTube on October 9, 2006 for $1.65 billion in Google stock.

*****

YouTube is an amazing resource. Whatever your mood, interest, or need, chances are, somebody has made a video to match it.

For example, while reading the first book in the Harry Potter series for the third time, I was rudely jerked out Harry's cupboard beneath the stairs by a loud grinding sound.

"What?" I screamed from the bathroom.

"The washing machine is busted," my wife shouted back.

Nice. Murphy's Law strikes again. Just when I had drained the last few hundred bucks out of my account for a new chainsaw, the washing machine goes on the fritz, threatening the precarious economic balance of my manhood.

"Don't worry," my wife shouted through the bathroom door. "I'm going to watch a YouTube video on it."

My brain was suddenly awash with images of an over flowing washing machine and death by electrocution. I grew up believing in Clint Eastwood's famous admonition, "A man's gotta know his limitations."

When it came to appliance repairs, I was extremely limited.

Four minutes later my wife tapped on the bathroom door.

"I know what the problem is. We have to replace the agitator dogs."

Agitator dogs? I agree, most dogs are agitating, but how did that relate to my broken washing machine?

As it turns out, the agitator dogs on a washing machine are small nylon cogs located at the top of the agitator. They're meant to wear out and cause distress among housewives and repair challenged husbands. In technical terms, engineers call this *planned obsolescence*, with the object being the subsequent purchase of a new machine.

After watching a two minute YouTube video on how to replace the dogs, I agreed that even with my limited skillset in all things appliance related, this was something I could do.

A six dollar part and twelve minutes of labor saved me the price of a new washing machine.

Thank you, YouTube. It looks like I'll get to keep my new chainsaw.

Now, where was I? Oh yeah. Dudley is just about to stomp on the stairs above Harry's cupboard.

*****

No modern tribute to trivia would be complete without at least a nod to J.K. Rowling's magical world, captured in the seven book *Harry Potter* series. The titles, with year of publication, include:

- The Philosopher's Stone (1997)
- The Chamber of Secrets (1998)
- The Prisoner of Azkaban (1999)
- The Goblet of Fire (2000)
- The Order of the Phoenix (2003)
- The Half-Blood Prince (2005)
- The Deathly Hallows (2007)

*****

In the Harry Potter stories, the Beauxbatons Academy of Magic is set in a palace in France. Its school coat of arms features two wands on a blue field. Each wand sparkles with three stars. Beauxbatons is French for, *beautiful batons*.

*****

The Leaky Cauldron pub is the primary gateway to *Diagon Alley*. The pub is invisible to muggles, and is situated between a music shop and a bookstore.

*****

Severus Snape, Lily Potter, and Petunia Potter Dursley all came from the same small village, called *Cokeworth*. Snape lived on a muggle street named *Spinner's End*.

*****

Author J.K. Rowling was struggling to survive on welfare when her first Harry Potter book sold. Within a handful of years she became one of the wealthiest women in the world when Scholastic picked up the publishing rights to her books and spread her creation to an appreciative audience of children and adults from around the world.

Fight or Flight and the Art of Self Defense

Other than honey badgers, who love nothing better than a fight to the death, most animals, including humans, would rather flee than fight. That is, we tend to avoid conflict, and when our fight or flight instincts kick in, we instinctively look to the flight option before anything else.

And this doesn't make us cowards. It makes us survivors.

But make no mistake, even the weakest and most frightened animal on the planet will turn and fight for his or her life when backed into a corner. And most animals, especially humans, will ignore their fight or flight instincts and rush headlong into a brawl to protect somebody they love, or to preserve the life of a child.

While your deepest instincts may be more about survival of the species than survival of the individual, nature understands that to create life and sustain the species, you must first protect yourself. To that end, she gave us the ability to watch Bruce Lee movies, and to mimic his nose thumbing antics.

About 20 years ago I hit the pause button on my *Enter the Dragon* movie, turned off my VHS player, crawled out of my recliner, and enrolled in a taekwondo class.

Taekwondo is a Korean martial art, and literally stands for the "art of hand and foot." It is a very form driven martial art, and requires students to master increasingly complex combinations of kicks, blocks, and punches. Most taekwondo schools, or dojos, focus on the children and youth market. That's great. From my experience, the kids in taekwondo were almost across the board ahead of their peers in school, had more self-confidence, and were head and shoulders above other kids when it came to discipline.

But the adults in my class were not interested in learning about discipline. We wanted to know how to defend ourselves on the street.

During a practice sparring session, the class instructor did something he had never done before. He paired a middle-aged woman against a young man. We all watched in anticipation. The woman was a black belt and knew every move in the book. The man, on the other hand, was a red belt, several skill levels below his female opponent.

The opponents bowed to each other and assumed their fighting positions. The man, not wanting to go on the attack against a woman, took a defensive posture. The woman on the other hand went on the offensive.

Normally, we only used light contact in sparring sessions, but as the woman moved in against her male opponent, he invited her to give him everything she had. For three minutes she kicked and punched her male opponent, as he stood passively blocking the occasional punch or kick, and basically allowing her to go at him.

Technically, the female black belt knew everything there was to know about taekwondo. Her skills towered above those of her male opponent. And if this was an Olympic event, she would have claimed the Gold Medal.

But life and self-defense are not Olympic sports. There are no rules on the street. And there's no such thing as a time-out or a do-over. Back in the dojo, the woman's repeated assaults on her male opponent did little to change a simple biological fact…no matter how good you are at punching and kicking, if your opponent is twice your size and twice your strength, you're working at a severe disadvantage.

The man in this brief sparring session was not trying to hurt the woman. He was not a desperate thug in a dark alley. Nor was he a drug maniac, or a sex starved predator. Had he been the slightest bit motivated to hurt or dominate his female opponent, she would have been finished within seconds.

What she needed was something my dad called an "equalizer." In his infinite wisdom, my dad encouraged me and my brothers to fight fair, but if the chips were down or we found ourselves facing a much bigger or more dangerous opponent, we had to find an equalizer.

A big brother is an equalizer. A baseball bat is an equalizer. And in the right hands, a knife or gun is an equalizer.

The ranking female student in our class realized a simple truth—her skills and memorization of complex punch and kick combinations did not rise to equalizer status. She left the class in tears and never returned.

In many cases, people may be better served to learn how to properly use a stun gun or bottle of pepper spray. For the more determined, an investment in firearms training and a concealed carry permit, may be the ideal solution.

*****

In the right hands (suggesting training, practice, and the correct motivation), a gun is hands down the best equalizer on the planet. Apparently, many Americans agree with me, as the numbers below suggest:

- With less than 5 percent of the world's population, American citizens own over half of all the guns in the world.
- It is estimated there are 89 guns for every 100 citizens in America, but interestingly, only a quarter of Americans own guns.

- The average gun owner in America owns 3 guns.
- 14.5 million Americans have active concealed carry permits.
- It is estimated that legal gun owners defuse or stop up to 2.5 million crimes per year.

*****

Every state interprets your right to defend yourself and your property differently. Here are the three main laws to consider:

- I was once advised by a police officer that it was my duty to retreat from a conflict. What this means is that in any case, even at home, where you are confronted by the potential for physical violence, it is your duty to retreat, and not defend yourself. For example, if I am sitting on my couch watching *Days of Our Lives*, and a man knocks down my front door, it is my duty to run out the back door.
- On the other hand, "stand your ground" laws give all citizens the right to defend themselves where they stand. They are not legally required to back away or give themselves up to criminals.
- The castle doctrine is similar to the stand your ground laws. In this case, the castle doctrine states you have the right to defend your home against forcible entry…and God help anybody who attempts a home invasion.

Again, the laws in the areas of self-defense vary by state. Roughly 23 states have stand your ground laws on the books, but each case of using deadly force to protect yourself or your property may expose you to criminal and/or civil charges.

Despite the advantages of arming yourself against home intruders and street violence, there are times when knowing a martial art can come in handy.

Here are the top ten martial art forms, according to their popularity:

- Krav Maga (Israeli Defense Force)
- Boxing (Mike Tyson)
- Brazilian Jiu Jitsu
- Keysi Fighting Method (Batman)
- Jiu Jitsu
- Wing Chun (Bruce Lee)
- Aikido (Steven Segal)
- Karate
- Kickboxing
- Jeet Kune Do

And then there are the U.S. Navy Seals.

Seal stands for, "Sea, Air, Land." Their preferred method of fighting is the engagement of stealth, combined with advanced weaponry. Their favorite up close and personal weapon is the MK3 Navy Knife, by Ontario Knife. Step back a few feet or a couple hundred yards, and the Navy Seal will hit you with his firearm.

Here are the top four firearms preferred by Seals:

- .300 Win Mag (sniper rifle)
- M4 (5.56mm automatic rifle with collapsible stock)
- HK MP5N (9mm submachine gun)
- Sig Sauer P226 (9mm pistol)

And when the shizer hits the fan and the Seal must resort to using his hands, he deploys an arsenal of martial arts training that focuses on pressure points in the body. Navy Seals use a mixed martial art form that has evolved from Jujitsu, Ninjitsu, Kung Fu, Karate, Judo, Krav Maga, Muay Thai, Silat Knife Techniques, and Western Boxing.

*****

In pressure point fighting, the combatant, or perhaps even you, attempts to deliver a disorienting or disruptive blow to his or her assailant. This is not necessarily a knockout blow, just something that distracts your assailant and gives you time to mount a stronger defense, or flee.

The main pressure points in the human body are:

- Eyes
- Ears
- Temple
- Nose
- Chin
- Back of neck
- Throat

All of these pressure points tend to focus on the head. In an emergency, you may not be able to reach your assailant's head. In those cases, you need to deliver a blow to his groin, or sternum…both of which, in my experience, can be painfully distracting.

*****

In all things martial art, self-defense, and combat relevant, remember this simple rule: Weapons are meant to be felt, not seen.

Don't be flashy. Don't showboat. Don't brandish. When the need arises, be felt.

Pennywise, Pound Foolish

In 1943 psychologist Abraham Maslow wrote a paper on human motivation that revolutionized motivational theory and came to be known as Maslow's Hierarchy of Needs.

Simply put, Maslow's Hierarchy of Needs suggests humans must first secure basic human needs, such as food, shelter, and love before the higher realms of self-actualization and happiness can be obtained. Short of trading a chicken for a personal service or pound of carrots, the quickest and easiest way to secure food and shelter is the exchange of money for goods.

No wonder money ranks at the top of human interests, and its pursuit consumes fully one third of our lives.

*****

Several years ago my wife and I were struggling to round up the funds for the next month's rent. Under-employed and highly unmotivated, I stumbled across a replay of an Oprah Winfrey show. Yes. I was that bored.

Long story made longer, Oprah was talking with a guest about a website called missingmoney.com.

Apparently, most states require lost and forgotten bank account balances, unclaimed insurance benefits, and abandoned security deposits, to be placed in an escrow account, pending their eventual collection by the rightful owners. The Missing Money website helps people find this money through a search engine feature that allows citizens to search for forgotten or lost funds online.

Later that day I entered my name in the search box. Nothing. Then I entered my wife's name. Again, nothing. Desperately disappointed, I entered my wife's maiden name and bam! She had an unclaimed life insurance disbursement from her deceased father. It wasn't a lot of money, but it was a gift from the money gods — and her very thoughtful father.

Check it for yourself. Go to missingmoney.com and do a search using every name in your family for every state you have ever lived in. If you find a match, submit a claim.

*****

Outside the rare opportunity to learn something juicy about their neighbor's sex life, nothing grabs and holds people's attention quite like money.

And it's just paper with portraits of dead white guys.

To paraphrase Thomas Jefferson, "government is the only institution on Earth that can combine valuable paper with valuable ink and make them both worthless."

But go ahead and try to convince your landlord it is only worthless paper.

Paper currency is known as *fiat money*. Its value lies solely in the trust of those people who trade it for goods and services. It is not backed by gold, silver, jewels, or oil.

The amount of currency in circulation (we're talking U.S. Dollars) is the total amount of cash in the hands of consumers and businesses. It is a component of the total money supply, which includes money held in banks and other financial institutions.

From an investor's or economist's perspective, the level of currency in circulation is an indicator of an economies health, because cash in hand is a critical factor in day-to-day consumption...which drives the Gross Domestic Product (GDP) numbers.

The current level of currency in circulation, of U.S. dollars, is approximately $1.2 trillion.

So, go ahead. Do your bit. The next time you're at the ballgame, buy that 8 dollar hot dog and 5 dollar soda.

Chances are, you owe a lot more money in the form of credit card debt, car loans, school loans, and your home mortgage than you have in savings or in your wallet.

Here are some money numbers designed to make you feel better about your personal debt according to a fascinating real-time ticker website called usdebtclock.org.

- The current federal government debt stands at $20.5 trillion, or roughly $63,000 per citizen.
- As of December 2017, the federal government had spent just over $4 trillion, and collected $3,5 trillion in various taxes and fees for the year.
- The U.S. government spends nearly $1.5 trillion per year on Medicare and Medicaid, and just under $1 trillion on Social Security.
- In 2017, the U.S. government spent $640 billion on defense.
- The combined debt of all U.S. households, business, and the government exceeds $68 trillion.
- The U.S. government currently employs 23,372,000 people. Wal Mart currently employs 2.2 million people…half of whom (based on the noise and activity behind my house) work the nightshift at my local Wal Mart Neighborhood Market.

All of the above numbers change constantly. For current real-time data, visit the usdebtclock.org site and see it for yourself.

Americans love to criticize government spending…especially when government contract and purchasing agents get caught buying $200 hammers and $800 toilets. The right to complain is in the Constitution, right?

But from the numbers below, it looks like Uncle Sam learned how to spend money he doesn't have from his millions of nephews and nieces.

*****

In the last official census (2010), 326 million Americans either filled in a form or allowed themselves to be counted as citizens.

Based on the number of homeless people who ask me for change every time I go grocery shopping, and the number of people who offer to do odd jobs for me whenever I visit Home Depot, I suspect the real population of America is closer to 360 million.

*****

According to the Bureau of Labor Statistics, 12,460,000 American adults are unemployed. This is the *actual* unemployed, versus the advertised *official* unemployed, 6,417,000.

*****

The current median income in America is $30,558. That means half of America earns more than 30K, and half make less than 30K...just slightly higher than inflation adjusted numbers for 1999 and 2007.

*****

The median price of a new home in America is $316,000. In the year 2000, the median price of a new home was $168,000.

*****

1.2 million people and businesses filed for bankruptcy in 2016.

*****

There were just over 604,000 home foreclosures in 2017...down significantly from the peak foreclosure years of 2008, 2009, and 2010 when the number of foreclosures averaged just under 3 million per year.

*****

42 million Americans live at or below the poverty level. Poverty in America is defined as a family of 4 earning less than $24,300 per year.

*****

41 million Americans receive food stamp assistance, and 165 million Americans receive free medical care in the form of Medicare, Medicaid, or various other programs for the uninsured.

*****

Americans hold $9.9 trillion in home mortgage debt, or around $137,000 per household owned. 63 percent of Americans own their home, with 19 percent of these people owning their home outright — that is, debt free.

*****

The median credit score for a new home loan is 754, with down payments averaging just over $12,000. Today's buyers typically put down 5% of the purchase price on a new home, compared to a median down payment of 20% ten years ago.

*****

Total outstanding credit card debt stands at $1 trillion, with an average family carrying over $5,000 in credit card debt.

*****

The median net worth of Americans aged under 35 is a paltry $6,676. The age range 65-69 has the highest average net worth at, $194,000.

*****

Government statisticians and economists love to use central tendencies to describe a set of data. The primary central tendencies are average, mode, and median. Each can be used to distort real data and create favorable impressions for the reporting agencies.

Whenever you see a central tendency, ask yourself why it is being used, in place of the other choices. Also, consider how outliers may be skewing this number, or distorting reality.

An *average*, or mean, of anything is simply the sum of all the data points, divided by the number of data points. For example, if five people took the same Civil Service exam, and their scores were 82, 90, 56, 73, and 98, the average is the sum of these numbers, 399, divided by 5, to equal an average test score of 79.8.

While as a group the average of 79.8 is a good indicator of test scores, it does little to accurately reflect the low of 56 and the high of 98. These high and low extremes represent what statisticians call, *outliers*.

The *median* on the other hand, simply finds the data point that best represents the middle point between the high and low data points. In the case of our test scores, if the numbers are arranged from low to high: 56, 73, 82, 90, 98, the middle figure is 82. That means half of all test results were lower than 82, and half of all test results were higher.

The *mode* looks for the most frequently occurring data point. For example, if 5 people scored 56 on the exam, and one of each scored 80, 87, 92, 95, 98, the mode for this data set would be 56. As you can see, this number totally neglects to recognize that just as many people passed the exam with flying colors, as they failed abysmally. Depending upon your objectives, the mode can cleverly paint the picture that everybody is a loser, while in actuality, only half of us are losers.

Again, when looking at aggregated numbers, think twice about what you are seeing, and consider the source. It's called *critical thinking*, and it is essential to making informed decisions.

But you knew that, right? After all, anybody who takes the time and effort to read books like this—even while sitting on the toilet—is serious about learning and understanding his or her world.

Congratulations!

You are an exceptional person.

14984536R00076

Printed in Great Britain
by Amazon